Finding
JESUS

written by **Christine Stevens Mower** & illustrated by **Kevin Keele**

CFI • An imprint of Cedar Fort, Inc. • Springville, Utah

Micah was seven. Well, almost eight!
His family lived in Judea a long time ago.

Micah was always full of adventure
and loved to learn new things.

One day, while he was out walking with his donkey, Dexter, he heard people talking about someone named Jesus. They were saying such amazing things!

Who was this
Jesus?

This made Micah so curious!
He wanted to see Jesus!
He wanted to meet Him too!

He decided right then, that very
day, that he was going to try to find
Jesus. Together, he and Dexter would
search until they found Him.

The next day, Micah and Dexter set out
on their journey to find Jesus.

They walked down lots of streets, but
they didn't see Him anywhere.

Soon, they got tired
and stopped to rest.

While Micah and Dexter were resting, a group of men walked by. Micah heard them say Jesus's name, so he quickly got up and followed them.

He overheard them tell the most wonderful story!

Later that night, while Micah was lying in bed,
he thought of the story he had heard.

*A nobleman of Capernaum had a son who was
very sick. He was afraid his son was going to die.
He heard Jesus could make sick people better.*

*The father quickly traveled to the city of
Cana where he found Jesus. He asked
Jesus if He would make his son better.*

Jesus told the father that his son would be healed. The father believed Him and left to go back home. When he got home, he saw that his son was healed, just like Jesus said he was.

Micah could hardly believe what he had heard. He was so happy knowing that the little boy was all better. Although he had not seen Him yet, Micah already loved this man called Jesus.

As Micah fell asleep, he decided that the next day he would try even harder to find Jesus.

When morning came, Micah and Dexter once again started on a journey to find Jesus. They walked all around town, up and down the streets, but still didn't see Him.

BUT . . . it was a great day anyway!
Do you know why? Because everywhere Micah
walked, he heard people talking about Jesus.

They were all saying how wonderful He was.
He healed and blessed people. He showed them
how to be loving and kind to everyone.

As Micah slowly walked home, he thought about what he had heard that day. He wanted to be like that!

He wanted to be like Jesus!

He tried to think of ways he could
help others, show love, and be kind.

As he continued walking, Micah noticed that a woman in front of him had dropped her baby's blanket. Micah hurried and picked up the blanket. He ran to hand it to the woman. She was so grateful and thanked him. It was the baby's favorite blanket.

Micah walked home with the
biggest smile ever!

When Micah got home, his friends were in the street playing stick ball. He tied Dexter up and went to join them. He was having so much fun. As he picked up the stick to hit the ball, he saw Leah.

Leah was shy and wasn't always included in the friends' games.

Micah took the stick, ran to Leah, and invited her to play. He was glad when he saw the big smile on her face.

Being like Jesus made Micah feel so happy!
He wanted to follow Him always!

Micah was so excited to start out once again
the third day to see if he could find Jesus.

After a while, Micah became sad and discouraged. He had been so sure he was going to find Jesus, but it still hadn't happened. With his head down, he sadly walked on, wondering if he would ever get to see Him.

Maybe, I should just go home, he thought.
But as he turned to leave, he found Him!

He couldn't believe it!

There He was! There was Jesus!

Tears came into Micah's eyes as
he slowly walked toward Jesus.

He loved Him so much!

Jesus looked right at Micah.

Micah couldn't stop himself. He ran toward Jesus as fast as he could.

As Micah ran toward Him,
Jesus reached out His arms . . .

. . . and lifted Micah
into the
BEST HUG EVER!

And then Micah knew,

JESUS
loved him
too!

Get the special companion song that goes along with this book!

"When I Follow Jesus," available on
iTunes, Spotify, Pandora, and YouTube.
https://www.youtube.com/watch?v=axoqnx6Strg

Download the sheet music at
www.christinestevensmower.com

With all my love, I would like to dedicate this book to my dear grandchildren,
and also to all children who want and need to feel the love of Jesus in their lives.
—Christine

Dedicated to my sons, Max, Jonah, and Christian.
—Kevin

ISBN 13: 978-1-4621-4482-2

Published by CFI, an imprint of Cedar Fort, Inc.
2373 W. 700 S., Suite 100, Springville, UT 84663
Distributed by Cedar Fort, Inc., www.cedarfort.com

Library of Congress Control Number: 2022949444

Cover design and interior layout by Shawnda T. Craig
Cover design © 2023 Cedar Fort, Inc.

Printed in China

10 9 8 7 6 5 4 3 2 1

Printed on acid-free paper